ADOLF HITLER

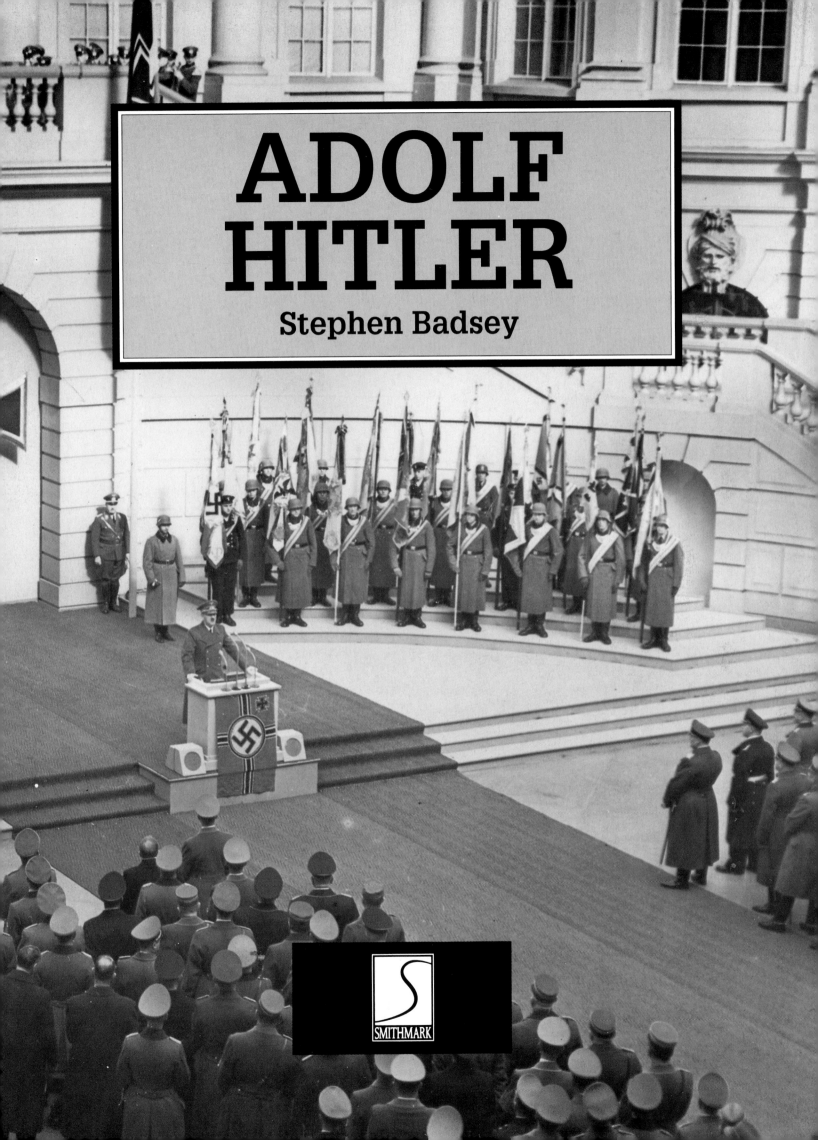

ADOLF HITLER

Stephen Badsey

SMITHMARK

This edition published in 1994
by SMITHMARK Publishers
Inc.
16 East 32nd Street
New York, New York 10016.

SMITHMARK books are
available for bulk purchase for
sales promotion and premium
use. For details write or
telephone the Manager of
Special Sales, SMITHMARK
Publishers Inc.,
16 East 32nd Street, New York,
NY 10016, (212) 532 6600

Produced by Brompton Books
Corp.,
15 Sherwood Place,
Greenwich, CT 06830

ISBN 0-8317-4210-0

Printed in China

10 9 8 7 6 5 4 3 2

EARLY LIFE
1889-1918

Adolf Hitler's origins were innocent enough. He was not a German, except in the same sense that a Canadian might be called an American. He was born an Austrian citizen and a Roman Catholic at 6.30pm on April 20th, 1889, at an inn called the *Gasthof zum Pommer* in the town of Braunau-am-Inn where his father was Inspector of Customs. But when Adolf was three years old his family moved to the town of Passau, where the River Inn joins the Danube. By chance the Austrian customs house at Passau lay within the town, on the German side of the border. Consequently, young Adolf grew up speaking German with the characteristic dialect of Bavaria rather than the cultured accents of Vienna.

Both Hitler's parents were from the farming region about fifty miles north of the Austrian capital. His father Alois was born in 1837, the illegitimate child of a peasant girl called Maria Anna Schicklgruber. Five years later, Maria Anna married Johann Georg Hiedler (another spelling of Hitler), but Alois kept the name of Schicklgruber until long after her death. In 1876 Johann Georg acknowledged himself as Alois' father, and he became Alois Hitler. It is likely that Alois' true father was the man who raised him, Johann Georg's brother, who spelled his name Johann von Nepomuk Hutler. The story that Hitler's real grandfather was Jewish probably has no foundation.

Despite his initial disadvantages, Alois Hitler worked his way up to become a senior civil servant, but his private life was a turbulent one. When his first wife died in 1883 he married his mistress, who was pregnant with their second child. When she in turn died soon afterwards he married in January 1885 his second cousin, Klara Polzl, who was 23 years Alois' junior and also carrying his child. Of their six children only the fourth, Adolf, and the sixth, Paula, survived to adulthood, together with the two children from Alois' previous marriage, Alois and Angela.

In 1895 Alois Hitler retired with his family to live near Linz in upper Austria. It was a grim household. Alois was intensely proud of his customs uniform and of his own rise to upper middle class respectability. He demanded 'correct' behavior from his family, reinforced by violent punishments. His elder son Alois ran away from home at the age of fourteen, leaving Adolf as both his chief hope and the target of his rage, while the ineffectual Klara convinced herself that her boy was in

PAGES 2/3: *Hitler speaks on Remembrance Day for Germany's war heroes, Berlin Arsenal, 1940.*

PAGES 4/5: *The opening of the first Autobahn between Frankfurt and Heidelberg in 1939.*

OPPOSITE: *Hitler as Chancellor of Germany addresses a Hitler Youth Rally at Nuremberg, 1934.*

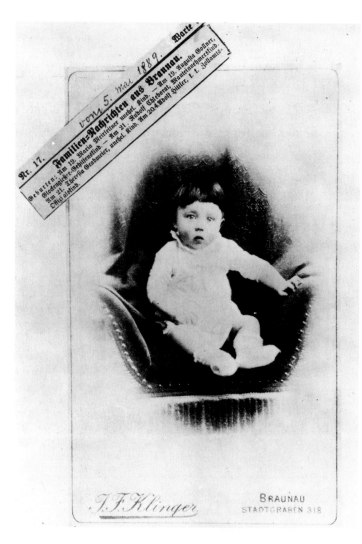

ABOVE: *The first known photograph of Adolf Hitler as a baby with (inset) the newspaper announcement of his birth.*

BELOW: *Hitler's school report card when he was 10. He attended three schools before the age of 11.*

RIGHT: *Hitler's mother Klara lived in awe of her dominating husband, always calling him 'uncle' even after their marriage. Her relationship with Adolf was very close, and he remained devoted to her after her death.*

poor health and needed constant attention. Adolf was educated at the local village and monastery schools, and when he reached eleven his father paid for him to attend *Realschule* or secondary school, so that he might also become a civil servant. The young Hitler was not, however, a success. He would later claim that he already wanted to be an artist, and that he deliberately failed his examinations out of spite for his father. He left school for good in 1905 without having attained the usual leaving certificate.

Alois Hitler died in 1903, leaving his family with enough money to live modestly without the need to work. When his mother, to whom he was devoted, died in 1907 Adolf moved to Vienna, where he had already tried and failed to enter the School of Fine Arts. His artistic talents were more towards draftsmanship than portrait painting, but the School of Architecture would not take him without academic qualifications. After a second rejection by the School of Fine Arts in 1908 he stayed in Vienna, living in hostels and earning his keep by drawing posters for shops and postcard views of the city for passers by. Although short of money, he had no responsibilities, nor any pressing need to find steady employment. He mixed with drifters and scroungers, with young idealists, with 'bohemians' in both senses of the word. Like many other young men in big cities he was often both poor and lonely, but despite later stories he was never really starving, nor was he ever a house painter.

Hitler's days were spent largely in idle talk. He neither drank nor smoked, and tended towards vegetarianism. He had few friends, being shy and awkward with both men and women, and he could become so violent in argument that others already regarded him as rather strange. He read widely but unsystematically, becoming passionate about social issues. He lost whatever remained of his religious faith, replacing it with a vague belief in a divine Providence. In Vienna his mind was filled with half-formed ideas on politics, philosophy and culture, a strong and rather tasteless brew from which the poison of his own beliefs was gradually distilled.

Twenty years before Hitler was born, 'Germany' existed only as the dream of the Pan-German movement to recreate the German Empire or *Reich* that had supposedly

ABOVE: *Hitler's junior school class in 1889. The ten-year-old Adolf is in the center of the back row.*

ABOVE RIGHT: *Hitler's registration card with the Vienna police in 1910, a routine document showing his occupation as 'Artist'.*

RIGHT: *A watercolor painting by Hitler of a Vienna street scene, done shortly before he left for Munich.*

FAR RIGHT: *A pencil sketch of a seventeenth century figure done by Hitler when he was eleven years old.*

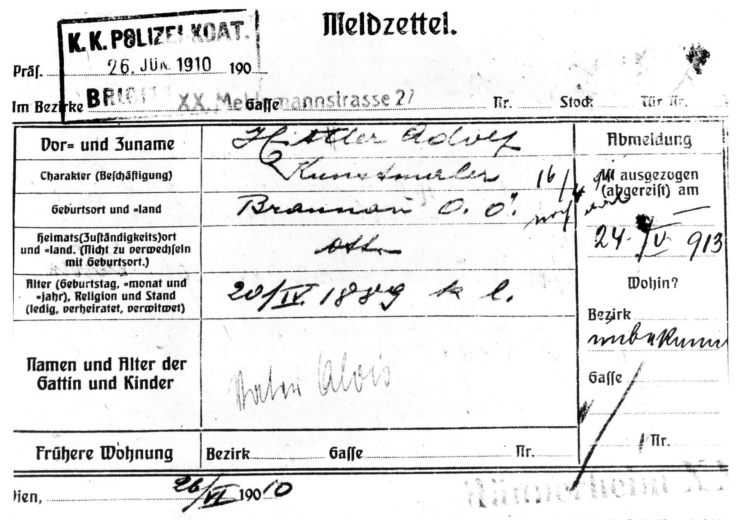

existed in Europe in medieval times. The most important German-speaking state was the Austrian Empire, with a majority of non-German subject peoples. Southern Germany was divided into several independent countries of which Bavaria – with Munich as its capital – was the largest. But in the Austro-Prussian War of 1866 Austria was defeated and its power eclipsed by the largely Protestant north German state of Prussia. The weakened Austrian Empire was forced to give Hungary its own internal government as part of the Dual Monarchy of Austria-Hungary. Soon the Slav peoples of Austria-Hungary were also agitating for their own self-government. Prussia and the south German states went on to defeat France, previously the strongest military power in Europe, in the Franco-Prussian War of 1870-1871. They then united without Austria into a new German Empire, dominated by Prussia.

The Pan-German idealists, of whom Hitler was one, admired Prussia and the new Germany almost beyond words. In its ruthless ambition and military might it seemed to embody the political philosophies of Friedrich Nietzsche (who finally went mad in the year Hitler was born). Simplified to the level of Vienna cafe talk, Nietzsche's central creed was that conflict was the chief source of human progress, and that great men should not

11

be bound by conventional ideas of good and evil. The major nineteenth century advances in biology, particularly Charles Darwin's notion that evolution was due to the competition of species, had also spawned the crank belief that humanity could be physically classified into superior and inferior types. In the Germanic version that Hitler learned, the *Herrenmenschen* ('Master Race') was represented at its most perfect by the tall, blond, blue-eyed Saxon or Prussian, known due to a ludicrous misunderstanding of prehistory as the 'Aryan' type, (the real Aryans lived in what is now Iran and Pakistan). Ironically, most of the eventual leaders of Hitler's Nazi Party were Austrians like himself and Adolf Eichmann, Bavarians like Ernst Röhm and Heinrich Himmler, or Rhinelanders like Josef Goebbels and Rudolf Hess.

Although in Hitler's racist view all non-Aryans were *Untermenschen* ('Inferior Races'), Negroes and Asiatics hardly entered his imagination, which was limited to his own middle European world. Slavs and Czechs he saw as barely human, but he reserved his particular venom for the Jews. In Germany and Austria anti-Semitism had only recently ceased to be 'respectable', and was still widely practised. Successful Jews had risen during the nineteenth century to positions of importance in industry, finance and the professions in the major cities, and cosmopolitan Vienna was markedly anti-Semitic (as was Berlin,

BELOW: *A newspaper photograph of the crowd in the Odeonplatz in Munich on August 2nd, 1914, cheering the declaration of war by Germany on Russia and France. Years later, after Hitler's own coming to power, he was identified among the crowd (center of the circled portion).*

RIGHT: *The early maneuver battles of 1914 soon turned into trench warfare for which neither side was properly equipped, and which kept the Western Front virtually deadlocked for four years. A pre-war German exercise is shown.*

BELOW RIGHT: *A British crowd outside Buckingham Palace cheering the declaration of war against Germany, August 4th, 1914. All over Europe people greeted the outbreak of war with similar enthusiasm.*

where over one third of Germany's 600,000 Jews lived). In Hitler's mind the figure of the Jew became the universal enemy – treacherous, lecherous, unspeakably evil, the source of all that was corrupt and wicked in the world.

Hitler the politician did not invent this unpleasant and dangerous nonsense, he was invented by it. His political ideas were unoriginal gatherings from the fringe right-wing radical parties of Austria and central Europe. His talent was for making the lie both popular and credible. Just as today, most people felt that much in the world was wrong, admired strength and success, and blamed their misfortunes on others not being more like themselves. Hitler took the people at their word, and shocked a world that thought it knew where the limits of human evil lay.

In 1913 Hitler moved at last to Germany, to Munich, to avoid the risk of conscription in Vienna. He was later judged to be physically unfit for military service, but he was not a coward. When the heir to the Austrian throne, Archduke Franz Ferdinand, was assassinated in Sarajevo on June 28th, 1914 by Slav terrorists, the First World War began. Hitler volunteered for the German Army, joining the 16th Bavarian Reserve Infantry Regiment. He made a very good soldier. For once his life had a purpose, and he enjoyed the comradeship, the danger, and the chance to wear uniform. Serving as a company runner on the Western Front throughout the war (except for a short spell in hospital 1916-1917) he won promotion to corporal and two Iron Crosses, one of them the very rare Iron Cross First Class. This was the happiest time of Hitler's life, and ever afterwards he believed that it had taught him more about the realities of war than his generals ever learned.

Germany fought the First World War as leader of the

ABOVE RIGHT: *Corporal Hitler (with the* pickelhaube *helmet) shares an underground dugout on the Western Front in 1916 with his comrades.*

RIGHT: *Hitler (back row, second from right without a cap) with a group of fellow wounded soldiers recovering at a field hospital after being badly gassed for the first time in the winter of 1916.*

ABOVE: *Captain Hermann Göring (right with cap), one of Germany's most decorated fighter aces of the First World War, who went on to become one of Hitler's leading supporters, with (center) Anthony Fokker, designer of the famous Fokker aircraft.*

BELOW: *Hitler (far right, seated) with fellow soldiers of the 16th Bavarian Reserve Infantry Regiment. It is worth emphasising that all Hitler's military service in World War I was on the Western Front. He never fought in the different conditions of Germany's war with Russia.*

ABOVE LEFT: *The terrible experience of the Western Front was never forgotten by those who served there. Here German wounded and prisoners are brought in by British troops during the battle of the Somme, 1916.*

LEFT: *British heavy artillery in the Battle of the Somme, in which Hitler also fought. The First World War was dominated by artillery, and it was a search for a less destructive way of fighting wars that led many, including Hitler, to the tank.*

Central Powers, including Austria-Hungary, against an alliance led by Great Britain, France and Imperial Russia. At first the war went well for the Germans, who seized part of northern France and Belgium and held it almost until the end. In November 1917 Russia collapsed in a Communist revolution (the 'October Revolution' by the Russian calendar) led by V I Lenin, whose new government made peace with Germany at Brest-Litovsk in January 1918. This settlement brought into existence something close to the Pan-German ideal of Greater Germany, stretching far eastwards into Russia. After more than three years of war the Germans appeared to be on the verge of total success. But this triumph lasted less than a year. An attempt to starve Great Britain by unrestricted submarine warfare had brought a declaration of war from the United States in April 1917, while the British naval blockade produced starvation and riots in German cities. After the failure of its last offensive in the west in spring 1918, the German Army was driven back steadily by the British and French, and by October it had acknowledged defeat. The war ended with an armistice on November 11th. The German Emperor, Kaiser Wilhelm II, abdicated and fled the country.

Germany lost the First World War because the German approach to conflict worked only for short wars against weaker, isolated, opponents. Total war required the complete social, economic and scientific resources of the

ABOVE: *The battlefield of the Third Battle of Ypres (Passchendaele) in 1917, another battle which Hitler experienced at first hand. It was scenes like these which convinced most of Europe that it should never again embark on such a war.*

country being organised alongside the military effort towards a realistic political aim. As the nineteenth century German military theorist Karl von Clausewitz put it, 'war is the continuation of politics by other means'. In Germany by the end of the First World War this position had effectively been reversed. The Army Chief of Staff, Field Marshal Paul von Hindenburg, dictated policy to the govern-

BELOW: *German* Stosstruppen *or* Stormtroopers *in 1917.*

ment, while his deputy, First Quartermaster General Erich Ludendorff, planned his battles with almost no political objective. Within the German Army, also, absolute priority was given to success on the battlefield. German generals were brilliant planners of battles and appallingly bad strategists.

Hitler, who had been temporarily blinded by gas in October 1918, was in hospital when the war ended. To him the defeat of Germany was devastating and incomprehensible. Hitler's view of war was naive and romantic. Throughout his life he admired the heroism of the warrior, the power of the general, the flashy uniform, the clever maneuver or technological gimmick, as if war were a game of skill played for its own sake. His hero was the eighteenth century Prussian warrior-king Frederick the Great. Like many Germans, he could not understand how, with its troops still everywhere on enemy soil, Germany could have lost the war. He grasped at the suggestion that

the German Army had been 'stabbed in the back' by the collapse of political will at home due to Allied propaganda, aided of course by Jewish financiers, left-wing revolutionaries and traitors. To Hitler, Germany had lost because its leaders had not been ruthless enough, both with the enemy and their own people.

The First World War ended with the Peace of Versailles

3063

in 1919, but in eastern Europe the fighting went on. Germany and Austria-Hungary were in chaos, while Lenin's Russia, renamed the Soviet Union, was committed to extending its revolution. Not until 1923 were the last disputes resolved. The final peace settlement was a mixture of the victorious Allies' desire to punish their enemies, their support for minority races and democratic ideals, and their conviction that war must never happen again. The League of Nations, a voluntary international organisation to settle disputes by peaceful means, was set up in Geneva. The new republics of Austria, Hungary, Czechoslovakia and Yugoslavia were created from Austria-Hungary. Germany remained precariously intact, but was forced to acknowledge that it had started the war (which was scarcely true), to pay reparations, to endure armies of occupation in the Rhineland, to give up its few overseas colonies and to reduce its own Army to 100,000 men with no tanks or aircraft. The Baltic states of Latvia, Lithuania and Estonia, together with Poland (which had not existed since 1795) had all fought their way to independence from Russia by 1921, and in order to give Poland a Baltic port a 'corridor' of land was established through to Danzig (modern Gdansk) cutting off East Prussia from the rest of Germany. Czechoslovakia also received the largely German Sudetenland as a defensible frontier. France took back the provinces of Alsace and Lorraine, absorbed into Germany in 1871, together with the largely German Saarland.

By 1918, even the victors were filled with horror at the cost, the suffering and the waste of the First World War. Most countries rushed to disband their armed forces and seek security in the League of Nations. The United States went one stage further, refusing to join the League and retiring to its traditional policy of isolation from world affairs. The British concentrated on their overseas empire, and the French, while suspicious of Germany, were unwilling to endure another major war. It seemed impossible that anyone could be so insane as to threaten the world once more with destruction on such a scale.

ABOVE LEFT: *A typically flamboyant set of gestures from one of Hitler's many powerful and effective* public speeches *denouncing the Versailles settlement after becoming Chancellor of Germany.*

ABOVE: *Watched by Allied leaders in the Hall of Mirrors in Versailles the German delegate signs* his country's agreement *to their peace terms, including an admission of Germany's war guilt.*

RISE TO POWER 1919-1933

After the Kaiser's abdication, Germany became a democratic republic, known as the Weimar Republic from the small town where it was proclaimed. As under the German Empire, the National Assembly or *Reichstag* governed from Berlin, while the old German states, including Bavaria where the king had also abdicated, retained their own assemblies and some internal self-government. Broadly Socialist and well-intentioned, the first Weimar government made itself unpopular by accepting the punitive Versailles settlement, and by failing to control the high inflation following Germany's defeat, which wiped out savings and led to mass unemployment. By 1922 the German mark was worth a hundredth of its 1918 value against the American dollar. As Germany plunged towards apparent revolution and disintegration, the *Reichswehr* or German Armed Forces, together with unofficial bands of ex-soldiers called *Freikorps*, took an ever greater part in politics. Assassination, intimidation and murderous street fights became the normal tools of government.

Corporal Hitler returned to Munich in January 1919. He was nearly 30 years old, in poor health, with no friends and no obvious future. In April 1919 the Communists proclaimed a Soviet Republic in Bavaria, only to be crushed by the Army and Freikorps, which set up a right-wing government. The Army put Hitler to work gathering information on revolutionary political groups in Munich. In September 1919, he joined the committee of the tiny *Deutsche Arbeiterpartie* (German Workers' Party), which he had been sent to investigate, and of which his friend Major Ernst Röhm was already a member. In February 1920 the Party's name was changed to *Nationalsozialistische Deutsche Arbeiterpartie* or NSDAP, shortened to 'Nazi' by its opponents. In April Hitler left the Army to concentrate on promoting the Nazi Party, of which he soon became leader. Many of his supporters came from the Bavarian government, from the Freikorps, and from the ex-soldiers' association *Stahlhelm* ('Steel Helmet').

Like the Weimar government, most European Socialists were moderate and democratic, claiming to represent the ordinary man against the aristocracy and big business. Even anti-democratic left-wingers like the Communists proclaimed brotherhood with workers in other countries. Some Nationalist groups, however, claimed to defend the interests of the German workers while rejecting both

OPPOSITE: *A propaganda painting entitled* Am Ausfang war das Wort *('In the beginning was the Word') by Nazi artist H. O. Hoyer showing the start of Hitler's political career.*

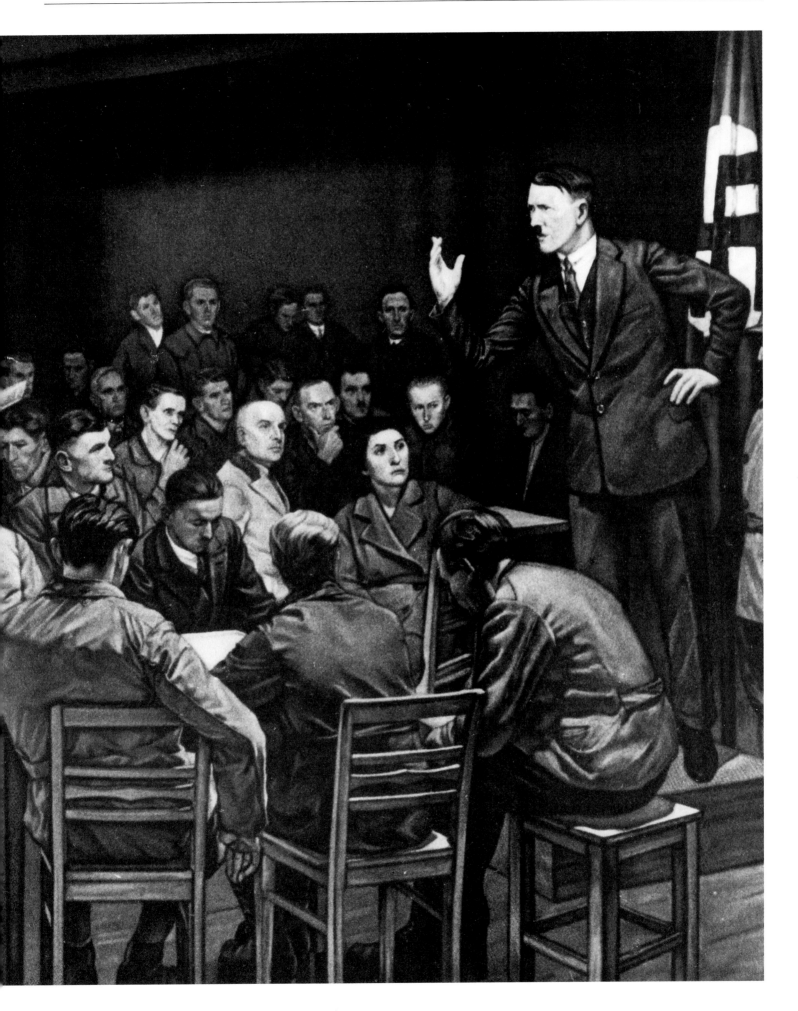

internationalism and democracy. This right-wing populism, or 'National Socialism', appealed to many Germans who felt that the rest of the world had cheated them and that Weimar democracy had failed. People like these made up the early membership of the Nazi Party.

Hitler proved brilliant at the seamier side of right-wing politics, which became an outlet for his energies and a substitute for all other passions. He advanced himself and his Party with all the skill, determination and will-power of the true ignorant bigot. Unaccountably, he also turned out to be a public orator of genius. No-one who heard Hitler speak, either to a mass gathering or face to face, ever forgot the experience. He developed a fluent, rhetorical style, full of irony and bathos, which left him physically and emotionally drained after each performance. He had no time for discussion or debate, nor was he particularly good at it. Within a year he was attracting paying audiences in their thousands to Nazi Party meetings, just to hear him speak. The Party gained members, including Captain Hermann Göring, a well-known First World War fighter ace.

Hitler was intent not on winning votes but on over-

ABOVE LEFT: *A headline from a Berlin newspaper dated July 28th, 1923, showing that the Dollar was then worth 1,000,000 Marks, reflecting the terrible hyperinflation of that year.*

LEFT: *Heinrich Himmler, one of Hitler's earliest supporters, shown (front row, second from left) with his class at the* Gymnasium *or high school in Landshut, Bavaria, to which he returned in 1919 after war service.*

ABOVE: *One of the Freikorps units of mercenary ex-Army soldiers stranded and forced to fight on alone in eastern Europe when Germany surrendered. Taken near Riga in May 1919 during the Russian Civil War.*

LEFT: *Troops loyal to the government keep order on the streets of Berlin during the attempted left-wing revolution in January 1919.*

throwing the Weimar Republic by a *putsch*, or violent uprising. In this the Nazis were greatly encouraged by a successful right-wing putsch in Italy in October 1922, when Benito Mussolini, a 37 year old former journalist, marched with his paramilitary forces on Rome and toppled the government. Mussolini called himself *Il Duce* ('Leader') and his supporters the *Fascisti* or Fascists (from *fasces*, an old Roman symbol of authority). The Nazis copied this shamelessly. Their paramilitary thugs, the SA or *Sturmabteilung* ('storm detachment' from the shock troops of the First World War) wore brown shirts in imitation of Mussolini's black-shirted Fascists and used their straight-arm salute. Hitler also called himself 'Leader' or *Führer*. The Nazi swastika, an ancient Aryan symbol, came from another Nationalist party.

In January 1923, in response to the Weimar government's failure to keep up reparations payments, French troops occupied the Ruhr, Germany's industrial heartland, and the German economy collapsed. From 400 marks to the dollar in 1922, there were 7,000 by February 1923, 160,000 by July, 1,000,000 by August and 130,000,000,000 by November. In Berlin and Munich a state of emergency was declared. Hitler saw this as his chance. His first attempt at a putsch in Munich on May 1st was a damp squib, but on November 8th-9th he tried again, this time with a respectable figurehead, the former First Quartermaster General Erich Ludendorff. The 'Beer Hall Putsch' (mounted from the *Burgerbraukeller*, the biggest beer hall in Munich) fell apart when a march by about 3,000 SA brownshirts led by Hitler and Ludendorff was fired on by police. The leaders of the putsch were arrested, while other participants such as Göring fled the country.

At the trial, Ludendorff was acquitted on a technicality, while the unsavory nature of Bavarian politics led to Hitler, who turned the court into a political circus, receiving the

ABOVE RIGHT: *Hitler as Führer of the Nazi party, September 2nd, 1923.*

ABOVE FAR RIGHT: *Hitler arriving with his staff for the Nuremberg Rally.*

RIGHT: *Revolutionaries marching to overthrow the government in Berlin, November 9th, 1918. The sign says 'Brother, Do Not Shoot!'*

FAR RIGHT: *Hitler watches the Nuremberg Rally.*

EXTREME RIGHT: *Hitler and Julius Streicher, one of his most extreme early supporters (on Hitler's right) watch the SA march past at Nuremberg.*

minimum possible sentence of five years. He served just under nine months of comfortable confinement in Landsberg Fortress, using the opportunity to dictate his political memoirs, *Mein Kampf* ('My Struggle'), to the young Rudolf Hess. It is hard to say how far this book constituted a real political program. Later, when trying to appear a respectable statesman, Hitler wished that he had never written it. In *Mein Kampf* he argued for war in the east to create a 'Greater Germany' or *Grossdeutschland* at the expense of the Soviet Union. The book also reaffirmed all Hitler's hatreds, especially against the Jews, and against the Communists whom he saw as part of the Jewish conspiracy. *Mein Kampf* sold over 300,000 copies before 1933, enabling Hitler to live on the proceeds.

On his release Hitler was banned from public speaking and the Nazi Party briefly outlawed. Hitler refounded the Party in February 1925 with a membership of fewer than 30,000. In February 1926 he did deals to win the support of his chief rivals for the Nazi leadership, Josef Goebbels and Gregor Strasser. Goebbels proved unusually gifted at organising publicity, and with his backing Hitler once more began to attract wider interest. In 1927, the year that Göring returned to Germany, the *Hitler Jugend* (Hitler Youth) was founded and the first mass rally held at Nuremberg. A year later, Hitler put Goebbels in full charge of Nazi propaganda.

When the Weimar President, Friedrich Ebert, died in

1925 the Nazis put up Ludendorff as a candidate, but withdrew their support when a better alternative presented itself in Ludendorff's former commander, Field Marshal Paul von Hindenburg, who became President with the support of almost all the Nationalist parties. With von Hindenburg as a figurehead, the German economy began temporarily to recover. Inflation eased, the problem of reparations was solved by international agreement, real wages rose, and in 1928 unemployment dropped below one million for the first time. Meanwhile, Germany was accepted back into the international community, joining the League of Nations in 1926. Two years later Germany became one of 65 countries to sign the Kellogg-Briand Pact, renouncing war as an instrument of policy; and in 1930, on condition that no German troops were ever stationed in the Rhineland, the last French soldiers left German soil.

After the Beer Hall Putsch, Hitler accepted that politics rather than force was the way to power. This meant doing deals with the other Nationalist parties, with big business, with the landowners and agricultural lobby, and with the Army. It also meant giving up the Nazi Party's revolutionary past and brutal image. The SA, although still valuable for street fights and intimidation, was too independent and devoted to the putsch for Hitler's new style. In 1928 he appointed Heinrich Himmler, an almost pathologically loyal SA member, to head his small personal bodyguard,

LEFT: *SA Stosstruppen of Göring's command preparing for the Beer Hall Putsch.*

BELOW: *Nine of the ten leaders of the Beer Hall Putsch who stood trial for high treason, with their lawyers and advisers: Hitler (6), Ludendorff (5) and Röhm (8), with Colonel Hermann Kriebel (4) and Lieutenants Bruckner (7), Wagner (9) and Pernet (1) of the SA, Nazi organiser Dr Friedrich Weber (2) and Munich Deputy Police Chief Wilhelm Frick (3).*

FAR LEFT: *Heavily armed SA members in Neustadt during the failed 1923 putsch. Private armies such as the SA were common in Germany at the time.*

LEFT: *Hitler entering Landsberg Fortress to start his term in prison. Loyal Nazis such as Rudolf Hess and Emil Maurice served in prison with him to write down his political memoirs.*

LEFT: *Heinrich Himmler carrying the banner, an Imperial German flag, for Ernst Röhm's* Reichskriegsflagge *unit of the SA during the Beer Hall Putsch, an episode which was to enter Nazi Party mythology.*

the black-shirted SS (*Schutzstaffeln* or 'protection squads'), which Himmler developed into Hitler's private army. Hitler also convinced Röhm, who had emigrated, to return to Germany in 1930 and take over command of the SA for him.

Hitler was not a German citizen, and could not run for office in Germany. He renounced his Austrian citizenship in 1925, leaving himself legally stateless, and in 1928 he moved from Munich to Berchtesgaden in the Bavarian Alps, where his elder sister Angela kept house for him. Nearly forty years old, Hitler fell in love with Angela's elder daughter, Geli Raubal, but the relationship proved a difficult one, and she was found shot dead, probably suicide, two years later. Shortly afterwards Hitler struck up a relationship with Eva Braun, a Munich shopgirl, who became his mistress and took over the running of his house in 1936. Hitler liked the company of women, of children, and of dogs. He seems to have tolerated, rather than in-

dulged, the strong homosexual element within the Nazi Party, which included Röhm. His private weaknesses, apart from a growing hypochondria, were for chocolate cake, pulp westerns and Wagner. Otherwise, politics and power consumed his life.

As Germany prospered, support for the Nazis dwindled almost to nothing. Membership stood in 1928 at 108,000, but in the May elections the Party polled only 2.5 percent of the vote, losing 20 of its 32 seats in the Reichstag. Even the Communists did better with 54 seats. Hitler's chance came with the Wall Street Crash of October 1929, which plunged the world into a deep depression. The Weimar economy depended heavily on overseas loans, and by

ABOVE: *Landsberg Fortress Prison.*

LEFT: *Hitler in his cell at Landsberg. He was allowed books and papers, visitors and his own clothes.*

FAR LEFT: *The respectable politician – Hitler's new image after the failure of the Beer Hall Putsch.*

RIGHT: *Hitler's departure from Landsberg, December 20th, 1924. This photograph has been retouched and may be a partial fake.*

ABOVE: *The Nazis were not the only ones to make use of propaganda photographs. On October 11th, 1931 Hitler met with other right-wing extremist leaders, including Alfred Hugenberg of the German Nationalist Party (left) to form the 'Harzburg Front' in opposition to the Weimar government. This picture has been faked by Hitler's opponents to show him with Hugenberg and Prince Eitel Friedrich (center), in order to suggest that Hitler meant to restore the monarchy.*

December there were two million Germans out of work. In March 1930 the coalition government fell apart, and the Chancellor, Hermann Müller, was granted emergency powers by von Hindenburg to rule by direct decree. In September his successor, Heinrich Brüning, called an election in the hope of winning an outright majority. By now, the Nazis looked increasingly attractive both to ordinary voters and to industrial magnates afraid of Communism and the trade unions. With financial backing from these industrialists, the Nazis took a third of the electoral votes, and 107 out of 491 Reichstag seats.

Brüning continued to rule by decree and with the support of the Socialist parties, who saw him as a lesser threat than Hitler. But as the depression deepened German banking houses failed, and at the end of 1931 over six million people, one quarter of the German workforce, were unemployed. Street battles between the SA and paramilitary groups from other parties, the Communist *Rotfrontkampferbund* and the Social Democrats' *Reichsbanner*, became commonplace. In the first half of 1931 over 200 political murders took place in public. The Army, faced once more with the prospect of keeping order, also began to take Hitler seriously. In March 1932, after hastily taking German citizenship, Hitler stood against von Hindenburg as President. Contriving to make even the 84-year-old 'father of Germany' look unpatriotic for supporting Brüning, Hitler forced the election to a second ballot. Von Hindenburg won with 19,250,000 votes, but an impressive 13,500,000 votes went to Hitler.

TOP LEFT: *The first of the big Nazi Party Nuremberg Rallies in 1927. These events were to become a byword for display and spectacle.*

ABOVE: *Propaganda chief Josef Goebbels (right) watches anxiously with Hitler at a Party Rally in Stuttgart, 1933.*

FAR LEFT: *Hitler with one of the Nazi 'old guard', Major General Franz Ritter von Epp, in 1929. Röhm's old Army commander, von Epp went on to become Nazi ruler of Bavaria in 1934.*

LEFT: *Another Nazi stunt: Hitler visits the memorial to the German dead of the 1914 Battle of Tannenberg in 1931.*

Brüning could not survive this. In June, after trying to ban the Nazi SA brownshirts, now 300,000 strong, he was brought down by an alliance of Nationalist politicians, landowners, Army officers and industrialists orchestrated by the new Defense Minister, General Kurt von Schleicher, who put in his place the right-wing Catholic Franz von Papen. The situation was perfect for the gutter politics at which Hitler excelled, this time with Germany itself as the prize. It was a shameful position for a great country to be in, and it produced a shameful result. The ban on the brownshirts was lifted, and in the July elections the Nazis secured over 37 percent of the vote and 230 seats as the largest single party in the Reichstag.

Refused the Chancellorship by von Schleicher and von Papen, Hitler proceeded to wreck the workings of the Reichstag, aided by Göring as Speaker. Like his predecessors, von Papen governed briefly by decree, and in November called another election. The Nazis did worse than before with 196 seats, but still remained the largest single party. In December von Schleicher himself took over as Chancellor from von Papen, trying to split the Nazis by offering Gregor Strasser the Vice-Chancellorship. At this political crisis of his career Hitler kept his grip and his nerve. Meanwhile von Papen, backed by the leading industrialists, attempted to return to power. Convinced that

RIGHT: *Josef Goebbels delivers a public speech during the 1930 election campaign.*

FAR RIGHT: *Despite his revolutionary politics, Hitler enjoyed very ordinary and old-fashioned pleasures, and visitors to Berchtesgaden found his home life surprisingly dull. Here he poses for the camera during a walk in the woods.*

BELOW: *A party to celebrate the reopening of the refurbished Nazi Party headquarters in Munich at the* Braun Haus, *January, 1st, 1931. Party Treasurer Franz Xavier Schwarz is next to Hitler (center) with glasses.*

RIGHT: *On the verge of power. A typically aggressive pose during a Nazi Party Day Rally in Weimar itself, October 1930.*

35

RIGHT: *A Nazi Party Rally through the little town of Braunschweig, just east of Hannover, in 1931. This kind of massive spectacle impressed and overawed many provincial German voters.*

RIGHT: *SA brownshirts, now numbering 300,000, march past the waiting Hitler during the Rally in Braunschweig. This kind of provocative display often led to street battles with rival paramilitary groups.*

BELOW: *But the Nazi Party saved its greatest efforts for the annual Nuremberg Party Day Rally. For this meeting in 1933, SA members from all over Germany pack the Leopold Hall to hear Hitler speak.*

BELOW RIGHT: *Josef Goebbels watches a parade during one of the Nuremberg Rallies. Black shirted SS are becoming as prominent as SA brownshirts. Also present (left in civilian clothes) is Franz von Papen.*

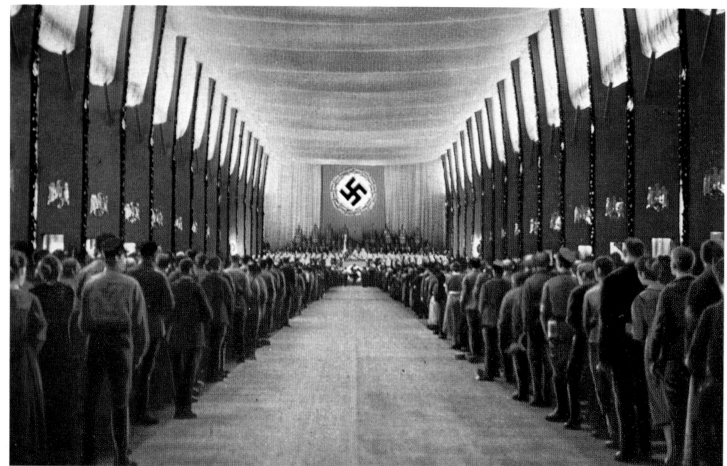

ABOVE LEFT: *Nazi campaign headquarters in Berlin during the July 1932 elections. Center are Himmler, von Epp and Röhm.*

LEFT: *Rival party posters during the 1932 elections.*

BELOW: *Hitler with Viktor Lutze, Röhm's replacement as head of the SA.*

LEFT: *The Nazi delegates to the 1932 Reichstag.*

BELOW: *Hitler's first public speech after his appointment as Chancellor January 30th, 1933.*

BOTTOM: *Hitler and von Papen on board the Chancellor's private Junkers Ju 52 aircraft.*

he could control Hitler, he persuaded the nearly senile von Hindenburg to give Hitler what he wanted, the Chancellorship, as part of a Nationalist coalition. On January 30th, 1933 von Hindenburg appointed Hitler as Chancellor of Germany.

Under the Weimar constitution, Hitler's appointment was perfectly legal and proper, no matter what his supporters were doing on the streets. As part of the agreement with von Papen his new cabinet contained only three Nazis out of twelve members. Von Papen himself became Vice-Chancellor, and Minister-President of Prussia with Göring as his Interior Minister. New elections were set for March 5th, and there were hopes that Nazi support would decline as before. Then, on the evening of February 27th, a fire broke out in the Reichstag building and it burned to the ground. A Dutchman called Marinus van der Lubbe was arrested and tried for the fire, claiming to have acted on his own.

How the 'Reichstag Fire' started remains a mystery. Hitler and the Nazis portrayed it as the start of a Communist uprising to topple the state. On the following morning, von Hindenburg signed a declaration allowing the government emergency powers of arrest. Göring, who had already packed the Prussian police force with Nazis, deputised 25,000 SA brownshirts and 15,000 SS stormtroopers as auxiliary policemen, and rounded up Communists, Socialists and other enemies of the Nazi Party. The March 5th elections took place amid confusion, hysteria, terror and violence. Altogether 89 percent of the electorate voted, and the Nazis received 44 percent of these votes, or 17,300,000, giving Hitler 288 out of 647 Reichstag seats, not quite enough for an outright majority. Hitler overcame this by a quick deal with the 52 Catholic Center Party deputies, and by declaring the election of 81 Communists invalid. On March 23rd, after solemn promises of good behavior by Hitler, the Reichstag passed by 441 to 94 votes an 'Enabling Act' allowing him to govern by decree for four years, and including the right to change the constitution. The Reichstag never met again.

THE FUHRER
1933-1939

Immediately following the Enabling Act, the Nazis seized power in Bavaria and the other states of Germany. Göring took charge of Prussia, founding the *Geheime Staatspolizei* or State Secret Police, better known as the Gestapo. Goebbels was made Minister of Public Enlightenment and Propaganda, and newspapers that failed to follow the Party line were closed down. Trade unions were declared illegal and replaced by a Nazi 'Labor Front'. The Stahlhelm and the Freikorps were merged with the SA, which by the end of the year had 4,500,000 members. In July all political parties except the Nazis were declared illegal. Within a few years virtually every school or university teacher, every policeman and judge, every civil servant, was a Party member. At the start of 1934 the state assemblies were abolished and all power concentrated in the person of the Chancellor.

Hitler never formally dispensed with the Weimar constitution for his 'Third Reich', he simply ignored it. In 1935 single-party elections were held for a new Reichstag, but it met only twice in ten years. Even the cabinet rarely gathered in formal session. Instead, Hitler parcelled out or invented offices for senior Nazis as pieces of patronage. The resulting administrative chaos increased Hitler's own power as the only man who could referee the fights between rival empires. If he really needed something done, he would appoint one or another favorite to a special role with 'full powers' to overcome the government obstacle course he had himself created. By 1936 Heinrich Himmler, head of the SS, controlled all German police including the Gestapo and the SD (*Sicherheitsdienst* or Security Service of the SS). In 1939 he became 'Reich Commissioner for the Consolidation of German Nationhood', in 1943 Minister of the Interior and 'Plenipotentiary for Reich Administration', and in 1944 head of all Intelligence organisations, leader of the *Volkssturm* (roughly, 'Home Guard') and commander of an Army Group. Göring became Minister-President of Prussia and head of the *Luftwaffe* (German Air Force) in 1934, and in 1940 was made Hitler's official successor and Germany's only *Reichsmarschall*, one rank higher than a field marshal.

In 1933, however, Hitler's position was not entirely secure. Originally the Nazis had been a party of the streets, with a radical social program. After Hitler's rise to power many Nazis, particularly the SA under Röhm, called for a 'second revolution' to carry out their original National Socialist aims. The Army disliked the SA, and

LEFT: *A Nazi recruiting poster for the* Hitler Jugend, *'Youth Serves The Leader – all ten year-olds into the Hitler Youth'. The Nazis often portrayed themselves as the party of youth and of the future, to break with the defeat and hopelessness of the Weimar years, and appeal to the young of Germany.*

Röhm's uncompromising stance became an embarrassment to Hitler. On June 30th, 1934, the 'Night of the Long Knives', Himmler's SS arrested and executed Röhm and the other SA leaders, together with General von Schleicher, Gregor Strasser, and altogether more than 80 of Hitler's rivals.

On August 2nd, 1934 von Hindenburg died of old age, and Hitler at once combined the office of President with those of Chancellor and Commander-in-Chief under the title *Führer und Reichskanzler*. On August 19th the German people were allowed to vote in a plebiscite on this. Of 45,500,000 enfranchised voters just under 2,000,000 did not vote, 870,000 ballot papers were spoiled, and 4,250,000 voted against Hitler. But over 38,000,000 Germans, a fraction under 90 percent of those voting, gave Hitler their approval. As happens when people do something of which they are later deeply ashamed, this vote was explained away as the effect of propaganda and intimidation. Certainly, the Nazis never won an outright majority in an election before 1934, but in later plebiscites and elections they always secured at least 90 percent of the vote. Hitler was enormously popular in Germany until at least the middle of the Second World War, and to the very end German opposition to his rule was minimal.

This popularity was largely due to Germany getting what it wanted and needed most, an end to the unemployment and poverty of the Weimar years. Hitler liked grandiose displays, impressive engineering, and complex

FAR LEFT: *The Nazi Party official newspaper* Völkischer Beobachter *for January 31st, 1933, announcing Hitler's appointment as Chancellor and details of his new Cabinet.*

BELOW LEFT: *Hitler with next to him Goebbels (left), Göring (right) and the rest of his new Cabinet, including von Papen (second far right).*

RIGHT: *On the night of his appointment as Chancellor Hitler addresses cheering Berliners from his Chancellery office.*

BELOW: *Communist Party 'subversives' are rounded up by SA special police on the morning after the Reichstag fire.*

technology virtually for their own sake. He had the good luck that his personal tastes, even his dreams, contained the cure for Germany's economic ills. He was also still enough of a radical to give the new generation of unorthodox economists a chance. Restrictions on foreign imports and a massive increase in public spending, based on Nazi notions of German cultural supremacy, created jobs by the million. By 1936 unemployment had dropped to nothing and there was even a labor shortage, while the standard of living had risen dramatically. Many of the new posts were in government, to run the Nazi bureaucracy. Other jobs came from the construction of the *Autobahn* or highways, and from public building programs, a favorite of Hitler the draftsman. A particular Nazi project was the small, cheap motor car affordable by everyone, the 'people's car' or *Volkswagen*.

Hitler told the Germans that they were the Master Race, and they believed him. University students held bonfires burning 'anti-German' books, while their professors taught 'German science' and even 'German mathematics'. Hitler Youth members betrayed their parents and schoolteachers to the Gestapo. Women dressed up for 'ancient Aryan' cultural displays, and men flocked to wear Nazi uniform. German National Socialism was not a properly thought-out system, it was an emotional outburst surrounding the personality of Adolf Hitler. It was for Hitler, not for the Nazi Party, that many Germans were prepared to die, and in the end National Socialism simply died with him.

Opposition to Hitler within Germany was difficult, very dangerous, and completely unprofitable. The cranks, the terrorists, and the madmen were now the legal govern-

LEFT: *After his appointment as Commander-in-Chief all German soldiers were required to swear an oath of loyalty to Hitler personally. The new Führer loved military parades, such as this one in Berlin in 1934.*

RIGHT: *But throughout Hitler's rule tensions remained between the* Wehrmacht *and the Nazi Party's private armies. Cyclist troops of the SA march past Hitler in Dortmund in 1933.*

RIGHT: *Although the power of the SA to oppose Hitler was broken in the 'Night of the Long Knives' it remained a formidable force. The Nuremberg Rally of 1934 was as impressive as ever.*

FAR RIGHT: *All over the country Nazi parades and displays impressed and intimidated the German people. Hitler in his brownshirt uniform takes the salute in Erfurt in 1933.*

ABOVE: *Hitler with Goebbels and Generalfeldmarschall Werner von Blomberg, his Minister of Defense, whose support within the Army was crucial to bringing Hitler to power.*

ABOVE RIGHT: *Another side of Hitler revealed in a propaganda photograph of 1935. In fact Hitler was very good with children.*

RIGHT: *In contrast to its reality, the Nazi state proclaimed social justice for all Germans. This November 1933 election poster shows von Hindenburg with Hitler. 'The Field Marshal and the Corporal – Fight With Us for Peace and Equal Rights'.*

ABOVE RIGHT: *Despite the extreme risks, some high-ranking Germans continued to oppose Hitler. Sitting next to him at this formal ceremony in Leipzig in 1934 is Mayor Karl Goerdeler, who helped organise a plot to overthrow Hitler in 1938 and another to assassinate him in 1944, for which he was hanged by the Nazis.*

RIGHT: *Hitler with the Italian dictator Benito Mussolini in 1934.*

FAR RIGHT: *Members of the SA display their loyalty to Hitler at the 1934 Nuremberg Rally, a few months after the 'Night of the Long Knives'.*

TOP, FAR LEFT: *Technology and aircraft were an important part of the Nazi image. Here Goebbels arrives at Königsberg airport.*

TOP LEFT: *Nazi ideology gave a very traditional role to women. Hitler talks with girls wearing peasant costume.*

ABOVE: *The opening of the first Volkswagen factory at Fallersleben in May 1938. Hitler promised a car for every German household.*

FAR LEFT: *SA men listen with rapt expressions as their Führer speaks.*

LEFT: *Hitler unveils his plans for the cities of the new Germany at an exhibition in 1938.*

ment. In March 1933 Himmler's SS opened the first concentration camp at Dachau near Munich. (Like 'propaganda', the term 'concentration camp' was an old one, and fairly innocent until the Nazis adopted it.) Hitler's opponents were sent without trial to endure squalid living conditions, brutal treatment and hard labor in the camps,. Indeed, lawyers could secure acquittals in the courts, only to join their clients behind the wire. By 1937 there were four camps with 35,000 inmates between them, and altogether 250,000 were arrested before 1939. The average sentence was three years, but many never left alive.

As well as political prisoners, the concentration camps held homosexuals and other 'social deviants', economic offenders such as black marketeers, and gypsies, who were regarded as a particularly 'inferior race'. The largest single group to be imprisoned were the Jews, the old Nazi hate-figure. The Nazi persecution of the Jews would have been considered harsh from the worst of the medieval tyrants; that it could happen in civilised, scientific, twentieth century Europe was at first unbelievable, and later almost too horrible to grasp. The world has never recovered from it.

The first Jews were sent to Dachau as soon as it opened, as the Nazis organised a boycott of Jewish shops and businesses. In November 1935 Hitler summoned his new all-Nazi Reichstag for a special session to Nuremberg, scene of the Party rallies, to enact the 'Nuremberg Laws'. These deprived German Jews of their citizenship, and made it an offence for them to marry non-Jews or to employ 'Aryan' women as servants. Jews lost their jobs and their savings, and were attacked or imprisoned at will by the SA and SS. This culminated in the *Kristallnacht* ('Night of the Broken Glass'), a full-scale attack by the SA in November 1938. Over 200 synagogues and 7,500 Jewish shops were burned, at least seventy Jews were murdered and 10,000 sent to concentration camps. To add insult, the Jewish community was fined and made to pay for the damage, a total of 1,250,000 marks. Behind the brutality, the 'Jewish question' was as confused and ill thought-out as the rest of Hitler's ideas. As well as being morally repugnant it made neither social nor economic sense, and the majority of Germans seem to have been indifferent to the fate of the Jews, rather than rabidly anti-Semitic. The Jewish community responded as it had done to persecution for centuries, by passive consent in the belief that the threat would pass, and that to fight back would be disastrous. The Nazis encouraged, and often forced, Jews to emigrate, but without their money. By 1941 there were only 165,000 Jews left in Germany.

Initially, Hitler's foreign policy was the same as the Weimar government's, to reverse the Versailles settlement and make Germany great once again. But he approached international politics as if Europe would fall to the same mixture of bullying, bombast and bluff that had given him Germany. At first he succeeded, simply because other governments were used to minimum standards of behavior, and because his threats of war scared a Europe for which the memory of the First World War was still too painful.

In 1933 Hitler took Germany out of the League of

ABOVE LEFT: *Old comrades from the Beer Hall Putsch who became deadly rivals: Himmler as head of the SS with Röhm just before the latter's death.*

ABOVE: *Sixty thousand members of the Hitler Youth parade before their Führer at the Nuremberg Rally, September 1934.*

FAR LEFT: *Hitler at the opening of the rebuilt* Reichsbank *with its president, Dr Hjalmar Schacht. An early Nazi supporter and Minister of Economics 1934-37, he later turned against Hitler and was sent to a concentration camp.*

LEFT: *Hitler's final triumph: the incredible pageant of the September 1934 Nuremberg Rally.*

Nations, and next year broke the Versailles treaty by announcing the expansion of the Armed Forces, renamed the *Wehrmacht*, and the creation of the Luftwaffe. In 1935 he obtained the return of the Saarland from France after a plebiscite, and in March 1936, against the advice of his generals, he moved troops into the Rhineland. Hitler's relations with the Army, still dominated by the Prussian aristocracy, were at best uneasy. As with economics, his enthusiasm for impressive machines and the unorthodox led him to favor generals who argued that tanks and aircraft were the future of war, against conventional military wisdom. But, despite the myth that Hitler himself did so much to foster, he kept much of the old military system, and did not put 'guns before butter'. Until well after 1939 the economy of the Third Reich was geared towards raising living standards, not war production, and economically it was incapable of fighting a long war.

In 1936 and 1937 Hitler told colleagues that Germany should plan for a defensive war by 1940, and an aggressive one by 1943. The object of the aggressive war was the Soviet Union, where Hitler wanted *Lebensraum* ('living space') for the people of his new German Empire, who would crush Communism and rule over the Slav races. Mussolini's Italy he saw as a probable ally, France as an almost certain enemy. One of his first acts in 1934 was to

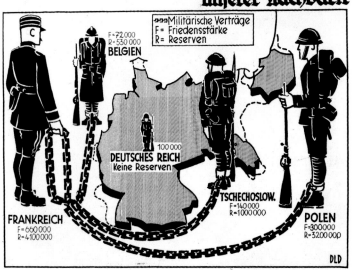

TOP: *Armored cars of the* Reichswehr *at the 1934 Nuremberg Rally. The Versailles settlement forbade the German Army to build tanks.*

ABOVE: *A Nazi propaganda poster showing Germany's weakness according to the provisions of the Versailles Treaty.*

52

ABOVE: *The 1935 Nuremberg Rally. With Hitler as Supreme Commander are (from left) Minister of Defense von Blomberg, recently appointed as Commander-in-Chief of the* Wehrmacht, *Göring, and General Werner Frieherr von Fritsch, the* Heeres *Commander-in-Chief. The German Army saw the Nazis as a way of restoring its old prestige and importance.*

LEFT: *Film director Leni Riefenstahl talks with Heinrich Himmler during the making of her famous documentary film of the 1934 Nuremberg Rally* Triumph des Willens *('Triumph of the Will').*

offer Poland a non-aggression pact, so splitting the 'Little Entente', the alliance of eastern European states led by the French. But the prospect of another First World War was too much for France even before Hitler. In 1934 it completed the Maginot Line (named after Minister of War André Maginot), a belt of concrete and steel defenses along the frontier with Germany, and based its strategy on defense. France not only would not, but could not defend eastern Europe. The obvious solution, an alliance with the Soviet Union under Josef Stalin, seemed out of the question.

The British were admired by Hitler for their empire, which he saw as a force of stability controlling the 'inferior races', and as Anglo-Saxons they almost qualified as Aryans. Despite the largest fleet in the world, they also possessed only tiny ground and air forces, and were even more determined than the French not to repeat the First World War. Hitler hoped for Britain as an ally, believing – as did some British politicians – that it could safely leave Europe to Germany. The United States, locked in economic depression and political isolation, was too remote for Hitler to care about for the moment.

The success of Hitler and Mussolini encouraged similar Fascist movements throughout Europe. In July 1934 Austrian Nazis attempted unsuccessfully to overthrow the government in a putsch, and in July 1936 Spanish Fascists under General Francisco Franco began a civil war against the Socialist government. While maintaining official neutrality, Germany and Italy sent 'volunteer' armed forces to fight on the Fascist side. The Spanish Civil War ended with a victory for Franco in March 1939, a few weeks before

Hitler's fiftieth birthday. Meanwhile, common interest brought Hitler and Mussolini closer together. In November 1936 Germany and Japan signed the Anti-Comintern Pact, aimed at the Soviet Union, with Italy joining a year later. The Berlin-Rome-Tokyo Axis was established, and in May 1939 Germany and Italy signed a formal military alliance, the 'Pact of Steel'.

Hitler's behavior placed an intolerable strain on the European state system. His destruction of German freedom made it hard enough for Britain and France to maintain good relations with Germany, but he failed to realise that if backed into a corner they would fight, however reluctantly, rather than see eastern Europe become a Nazi Empire. As in domestic politics, Hitler created the highly

FAR LEFT: *One of several treaties and agreements signed by Germany and Italy. Mussolini signs while Hitler's Foreign Minister, Joachim von Ribbentrop (right) looks on.*

LEFT: *German troops re-occupy the demilitarised Rhineland, March 7th, 1936. It is now known that Hitler would have backed down if Britain or France had opposed this move.*

BELOW LEFT: *Although much of German rearmament was a bluff, it could provide an impressive display. Hitler reviews SdKfz 231 armored cars of one of his five Panzer divisions, August 1938.*

BELOW: *The Versailles Treaty had forbidden Germany submarines (Unterseebooten or 'U-Boats'). In 1935 the British agreed to Hitler's creation of a new U-Boat fleet, which was also largely a sham, only able to keep a maximum 22 boats at sea at any one time until the end of 1940. This is U-52, a Type VIIB boat seen in 1938.*

ABOVE: *A wartime meeting in Germany of the Axis representatives on the anniversary of the signing of their alliance. Von Ribbentrop (center) with the Japanese Ambassador General Oshima Hiroshi (left) and the Italian Ambassador Dino Alfieri.*

RIGHT: *One of Germany's allies pays a state visit, June 1939. Prince Paul of Yugoslavia, flanked by Hitler and Göring (right), shakes hands with the Prussian Finance Minister, Johannes Popitz, at one of Berlin's stations. Note that Hitler is wearing his Iron Cross.*

charged atmosphere in which others made mistakes, and then exploited the results. In Austria, continued Nazi agitation led to a crisis meeting at Berchtesgaden on February 12th, 1938 between Hitler and the Austrian chancellor, Kurt von Schuschnigg, in which Hitler demanded the inclusion of National Socialists in the Austrian government. Von Schuschnigg tried to outmaneuver Hitler by holding a plebiscite on his government's future on March 13th, and Hitler, with Mussolini's support, threatened to invade. The Austrians caved in, von Schuschnigg was forced to resign, and the German invasion on March 12th turned into a victory parade as Austria was declared part of the Reich. As the *Anschluss* ('joining') with his mother country took place, Hitler promised Mussolini his eternal gratitude – one of the few promises he ever kept. Two Austrian concentration camps were at once established by the SS. A later plebiscite showed that 98 percent of Reich voters approved of Hitler's action.

Already Hitler had made his 'last territorial demand' more than once, and had formally abrogated the Versailles treaty in 1937. His next obvious target was Czechoslovakia over the Sudetenland. The British and French tried to head off the crisis, while still refusing to look at an alliance with the Soviet Union. At the Nuremberg Rally on September 12th, 1938 Hitler announced that his patience was at an end, and next day the Sudeten Germans rose in an abortive revolt. On September 15th the British Prime Minister, Neville Chamberlain, flew to Munich to see Hitler and agreed that Germany should have the Sudetenland. The 'Munich Agreement' between Germany, Britain, France and Italy was concluded on September 29th. The Czech President, Edvard Beneš, was not consulted. Chamberlain flew home in triumph, declaring, 'I believe that it is peace in our time'.

ABOVE: *Hitler and Chamberlain shake hands at the end of the second series of meetings which led to the 'Munich Agreement', Hotel Dreesen, Bad Godesberg, September 24th, 1938.*

LEFT: *The strain shows at the start of final negotiations at Munich, September 29th, 1938. Left to right are Mussolini, Hitler, his personal interpreter Dr. Paul Schmidt, and Chamberlain.*

Within a few months, 'Munich' was the dirtiest word in British politics. As German troops occupied the Sudetenland, the Slovaks also demanded autonomy, and what remained of Czechoslovakia became, briefly, Czecho-Slovakia. Even the Poles and Hungarians seized Czech territory in October and November 1938, and the country slid into chaos. On March 14th, 1939, Slovakia declared itself independent and asked for German protection. Next day, as the troops, the SS and the Gestapo moved in, northern Czechoslovakia was absorbed into the Third Reich as the Protectorate of Bohemia and Moravia. Slovakia kept its notional independence.

The British and French were now rearming as fast as they could, taking the measures for total war. After discussions with the Soviet Union, marred by mutual distrust, they issued guarantees of military support to Poland on March 31st. Czechoslovakia had been the strongest democracy in eastern Europe. Poland was at least as anti-Semitic as pre-Nazi Germany, and completely indefensible by any means Britain and France had available. The Danzig corridor was also by far the most legitimate grievance that Germany had. But as far as Britain and France were concerned, the issue was not Poland but that Hitler must finally be stopped.

By August, the Wehrmacht's plans to invade Poland were complete. Although Britain and France tried again for military support from the Soviet Union, the Poles themselves blocked the move. Stalin drew his own conclusions, and on August 23rd, in its most spectacular diplomatic maneuver, Hitler's government signed a treaty of non-aggression and friendship with the Soviet Union, and waited for its enemies to recognise reality. On August 25th

LEFT: *Although the Kriegsmarine expanded after 1936 it was still too small to be a major fighting force by the outbreak of war. As in many other things, Hitler preferred showy prestige projects to real strength in depth. Here he launches the Bismarck, which at 45,000 tons was, for a time, the world's biggest battleship, February, 1939.*

BELOW: *The moment in which the British and French at last realised that their attempts to appease Hitler had failed. German troops march into Prague as Germany annexes Czechoslovakia. March 15th, 1939.*

Britain signed a formal treaty of defense with Poland. Ignoring this, Hitler staged a small farce in which SS troops in Polish uniforms pretended to attack a German customs post, and on September 1st his troops crossed the Polish border. On September 3rd Britain and France declared war on Germany. No-one was more surprised or dismayed than Adolf Hitler.

LEFT: *A Jewish-owned shop in Magdeburg on the morning after the Kristallnacht, November 10th, 1938.*

ABOVE FAR LEFT: *Nazi persecution of the Jews. This Jewish-owned shop in Berlin bears Nazi posters calling for a boycott of all Jewish businesses by 'Aryans', April 1933.*

FAR LEFT: *Vienna Jews forced to scrub the sidewalks as an improvised humiliation before being sent to the camps, 1938.*

THE WARLORD 1939-1945

None of the countries which found themselves at war in 1939 was ready to fight. The Poles, menaced from three sides by superior forces, had no answer to the German armored *Blitzkrieg* ('lightning war'), or to the Soviet attack from the east which came two weeks later, and by October the fighting was over. But Hitler's generals were horrified at the prospect of confronting France and Britain. The Luftwaffe had no long-range bombers, the *Kriegsmarine* (Navy) had only 22 ocean-going submarines, and the *Heer* (Army) was smaller and had fewer tanks than its enemies. Meanwhile the French sat behind the Maginot Line, hardly daring to attack for fear of the Wehrmacht. The Royal Air Force's belief that it could bomb Germany in daylight was soon exploded, the Royal Navy was no more use to Poland than the Maginot Line, and the British Army was actually less well prepared for war than in 1914.

In April 1940 the Germans forestalled an Anglo-French attempt to move troops into neutral Norway by occupying it themselves, together with Denmark. The Allied failure brought down the British government, and on May 10th Winston Churchill became Prime Minister. Coincidentally, this was the day that Hitler had chosen for the German attack on France, together with neutral Holland and Belgium, based on an armored Blitzkrieg by-passing the Maginot Line and surrounding the Allied forces. Although numerically superior in everything but aircraft, the Allies collapsed beneath this German thunderbolt. Mussolini declared war on Britain and France on June 10th, and twelve days later France capitulated. The decision of Versailles was finally reversed. Except for a handful of neutral countries, Hitler was ruler of Europe from the Arctic to the Mediterranean. His greatest gamble, taken as usual against his generals' advice, had become his greatest triumph.

The Wehrmacht had done what it did best, winning short aggressive wars against hesitant enemies. It was the moment for Hitler to stop if he could. But although Churchill's government looked seriously at his offers, it would not make peace. The war against Hitler had become a moral crusade as well as a question of national survival. The German forces were completely unprepared to undertake an invasion, and after the Luftwaffe's failure to secure air superiority in the Battle of Britain, Hitler turned eastward. By late 1940 Britain was almost bankrupt, fighting

RIGHT: *The Victory Parade through the streets of* *Berlin to celebrate the defeat of France and the* *Western Allies, July 19th, 1940.*

RIGHT: *In keeping with Hitler's love of novelty and new technology, the* Luftwaffe *was the first force in the world to use paratroops in war. Here Hitler talks with two* Fallschirmjaeger pioniere *who led the capture of the crucial Dutch fortress of Eben Emael in May 1940.*

FAR RIGHT: *A study in faces as Hitler meets front line troops in Poland, 1939. Walking behind Hitler (with cap and goggles) is Martin Bormann who held an unofficial position (made official in 1943) as Hitler's Secretary and head of the Nazi Party organisation.*

BELOW: *General (later Field Marshal) Fritz Erich von Manstein, who as Chief of Staff to Army Group A in 1940 drew up the plans which led to the defeat of France.*

for its life in the Atlantic, with its main effort being made against the Italians in north Africa. But after the fall of France, President Franklin D Roosevelt put the still-neutral United States onto full war production, creating 'the arsenal of democracy' to supply Britain, the survival of which was never afterwards in doubt. Hitler, meanwhile, had forged a massive Axis alliance. In September 1940 Germany, Italy and Japan signed the 'Tripartite Pact', joined within a few months by Finland, Slovakia, Hungary, Bulgaria and Romania. Yugoslavia, which tried to back out of the Pact, was over-run together with Greece in April 1941. Finally, on June 22nd Germany, together with its European allies, launched an all-out attack on the Soviet Union.

This was Hitler's crusade, the war against Communism and the Untermenschen, fought for Lebensraum and the creation of Greater Germany. Hitler believed that Stalin's empire was as ramshackle as the old Austria-Hungary, and would collapse in weeks. The German Army had actually disbanded divisions and decreased weapons' production since 1940, and was not equipped for a winter campaign. At first 'Operation Barbarossa' made remarkable progress. After a month, Hitler's generals wanted to make straight for Moscow, the fall of which might have shocked the Soviet Union into surrender, but he overruled them, and by the time he changed his mind it was too late. Neither Moscow nor Leningrad had fallen by the winter snows. In Stalin, Hitler faced a dictator every bit

as ruthless as himself, considerably more able, and with far greater resources. After the initial shock Soviet troops fought hard for something older than Communism, for 'Mother Russia' in the ageless struggle of Teutons against Slavs. It was a war after Hitler's tastes, a war of race and of ideologies, brutal and barbaric. It was also a war for which Germany and its armed forces were poorly prepared.

Hitler still would not, or could not, put the Reich onto a total war footing. Production of weapons, tanks and aircraft in Germany rose only slightly over peacetime rates, and the output of consumer goods did not peak until 1941. In occupied countries, attempts at industrial co-operation were wrecked by the brutality of the Gestapo and SD, while in the east SS *Einsatzgruppen* ('action groups')

stirred up hatred with their tortures and executions. However, a surprising number of non-Germans did volunteer for the SS.

After his first successes Hitler came to think of himself as a military genius, and virtually gave up domestic politics, making only seven public speeches in 1940. For Barbarossa he moved from Berchtesgaden to his military headquarters at the *Wolfsschanze* (Wolf's Lair) near Rastenburg in east Prussia, and hardly left it for the rest of the war. In December 1941 the German line in the east cracked under Stalin's first counterattacks, and Hitler took control of the battle himself, dismissing commanders and ordering divisions about by telephone, finally stabilising the retreat about one hundred miles from Moscow. He sacked

RIGHT: *Hitler and his commanders at the surrender of the French forces, June 21st, 1940. Hitler chose the same railroad carriage in Compiegne forest at which Germany had signed the Armistice in 1918. From left, Field Marshal von Brauchitsch, Admiral Raeder, Hitler, Hess, Göring, von Rippentrop, with two of Hitler's aides.*

the Army Commander-in-Chief, Field Marshal Walter von Brauchitsch, taking his post while remaining Commander-in-Chief of the Armed Forces. From then on the Eastern Front absorbed nearly all his attention, and most of Germany's warmaking capability. The strain told, and he became a restless, lonely figure, unable to sleep, in real or imagined poor health, surrounded by soldiers and a tiny circle of functionaries who gradually became his only friends.

On December 7th, 1941 the Japanese attacked Pearl Harbor. In Hitler's eyes, the Americans were a rabble made up of the rejects from every race on earth, dominated by Jewish financiers and flabby with democracy. On December 11th he declared war on the United States in support of Japan. Over Christmas, the Americans and British agreed that their war effort would give priority to defeating Germany. Within a year, from his position as master of Europe, Hitler had voluntarily committed himself to war with the United States, the Soviet Union and the British Empire, between them the controllers of most of the world's shipping, industry, and oil. By late 1943 each of them was outproducing Germany in tanks and aircraft. As long as the fear and hatred of Germany created by Hitler held the Allies together, there was not the slightest doubt

ABOVE: *Hitler as Warlord. At a demonstration of a new tank with (left) his Minister for Armaments, Albert Speer.*

LEFT: *Discussing strategy with Colonel General Ferdinand Schörner (with glasses), later a Field Marshal and Army Group commander on the Eastern Front.*

FAR LEFT: *German armor bursts through the Ardennes forest and into France, May 1940. In fact these particular tanks are PzKpfw 38(t), built in Czechoslovakia and taken over by the Wehrmacht from the Czech Army in 1939.*

ABOVE: *One of Hitler's increasingly rare public appearances after the start of the war, at a funeral service for sailors from the pocket battleship* Deutschland *at Wilhelmshaven, 1940.*

RIGHT: *The wiping out of the shameful defeat of 1918 made Hitler immensely popular with the Army, and to the very end of the war its men fought with great courage and determination for him. Proud and happy soldiers of the* Heer *at the Victory Parade in Berlin, July 19th, 1940.*

LEFT: *Hitler shakes hands with Field Marshal Philippe Henri Pétain, the old French war hero who governed the puppet state of Vichy France in collaboration with the Germans after the surrender in 1940.*

BELOW: *Hitler during a visit by Turkish Army officers to the Wolfsschanze, July 1943. Despite German offers of alliance, Turkey remained neutral throughout the war.*

that he would lose this war. It was, as Churchill put it, 'merely the proper application of overwhelming force'.

Hitler the warlord had much the same abilities as Hitler the politician. He was good at the details of battles, and he became a walking encyclopedia of tanks and aircraft, but he knew no more about the higher direction of a war than about international relations or social justice, and his war effort showed the characteristic muddle of the Nazi state. It took the growing strength of the Anglo-American bombing offensive against German cities after 1942 to make him rationalise war production. Co-operation was minimal between the Army, the Navy and Göring's Luft-waffe, which controlled not only aircraft and anti-aircraft defenses but over thirty fighting divisions by the war's end. Similarly, Himmler built up the *Waffen-SS* ('armed SS') from a single bodyguard regiment in 1939 into a force of over thirty divisions, nine of them armored, and all largely independent of Army control.

Hitler applied the same 'divide and rule' tactics to the Army itself. After von Brauchitsch's dismissal, he used Army High Command (*Oberkommando des Heeres* or OKH) to run only the Eastern Front while Armed Forces High Command (*Oberkommando der Wehrmacht* or OKW) ran the rest of the war. He changed his mind and his generals at will; even Heinz Guderian, the creator of the *Panzer* (armored) troops, was sacked and reinstated three times from various posts. Hitler also created so many field marshals that the rank was seriously devalued, going to his favorite Erwin Rommel for commanding just three German and nine Italian divisions in north Africa. Most senior officers detested Hitler, but felt bound by the traditions of the Army and the personal oath of loyalty that since 1934 all soldiers had sworn to the Führer.

In April 1942 the Nazi Reichstag was convened for the second and last time to make Hitler *Oberster Gerichtsherr* (Supreme Lawgiver), giving his decrees the absolute force of law in Germany. Thereafter he virtually ceased to appear in public, devoting himself to his military maps. He

had finally grasped that a connection exists between economic strength and warmaking, and for a while he could think of nothing else. His 1942 campaign on the Eastern Front was launched not at Moscow but to secure the oil wells of the southern Caucasus. It is hard to separate fact from fantasy in his plans. After Stalin's defeat Hitler would occupy Russia west of the Urals, building great cities and super-highways running from Norway to the Crimea. Next, Britain with its fleet and empire would join the Reich. German forces would drive through the Caucasus and Middle East into India, linking up with the Japanese. Finally would come a showdown with the United States, and world domination. The whole grandiose conception hit reality at Stalingrad (modern Volgograd), where after months of bitter fighting German forces were crushed into surrender on January 31st, 1943. Meanwhile the British had pushed Rommel out of Egypt in October 1942; next month they and the Americans landed in Morocco and

LEFT: *Hitler in 1943, at home in Berchtesgaden, a 'home' that he visited less and less as the war went on.*

ABOVE RIGHT: *Stalin's Foreign Minister, V. M. Molotov (left) speaks with Hitler through an interpreter, Berlin, November 1940. Despite their 1939 agreement, Stalin and Hitler were deeply suspicious of each other. In the event, Hitler attacked first.*

CENTER RIGHT: *Winter conditions on the Eastern Front. The German Army was completely unequipped for its first war winter. All through the war, most German military transport was horse-drawn as shown.*

BELOW RIGHT: *Senior SS men who ran the death camps for Hitler. From left, Reinhard Heydrich, Himmler's deputy and head of the SD until his assassination in Prague in 1942; Karl Adolf Eichmann, head of the Gestapo Jewish Bureau; Rudolf Franz Höss, Commandant of Auschwitz extermination camp; Josef Kramer, Commandant of Belsen camp.*

Algeria; and by May 1943 the only Axis forces left in north Africa were prisoners.

After Stalingrad, Hitler was never the same again. He knew, as did his generals, that the war was lost, but he could not give it up, declaring that the German people must fight or die. In 1943 the Allies announced a policy of unconditional surrender for Germany, and this together with faith in the Führer, fear of the Gestapo and their own determination (actually strengthened by Allied bombing) kept the German people fighting to the very end. As they did so, they became accomplices to perhaps the greatest crime the world has ever known.

Before the war Europe had roughly seven million Jews, three million of them living in Poland. In October 1940 the Nazis forced 500,000 Warsaw Jews into a walled ghetto in conditions of appalling squalor and starvation. Next spring, Hitler ordered that throughout eastern Europe groups previously sent to concentration camps were instead to be shot. SS Einsatzgruppen carried out the task, murdering, for example, over 100,000 Jews and other 'undesirables' at Babi Yar near Kiev in September 1941. In January 1942 the 'Final Solution' to the Jewish problem was declared. At the war's start the SS had killed off nearly 90,000 mentally ill and handicapped Germans by poison

AT THE HISTORY LESSON
Cartoon by Efimof, 1941

gas as 'useless mouths', and now the same method was used to exterminate the Jews of Europe, who were rounded up from occupied countries and shipped to extermination camps in the east. In April 1943 the surviving population of the Warsaw ghetto rose in revolt, and was wiped out. Others died of suffering and starvation in the concentration camps. In November 1943 Greater Germany was declared free of Jews, although the organised murder continued for another year. Even in this unspeakable act there was the usual Nazi muddle, with political fights between those who wanted Jews used as slave labor and those who simply wanted them dead. A handful of Jews also survived by various methods, including blind chance. But about six million died, along with an equal number of non-Jewish 'enemies of the Reich', two million of them children.

Hitler himself played little direct part in the mass murder conducted in his name. As the war went on, he disappeared increasingly into a world of military fantasy, putting his faith in the example of Frederick the Great, remembered in German history for surviving a seemingly hopeless military situation in 1759, and in the technological quick fix. Germany produced the biggest tank of the war, the first jet and rocket-propelled fighters, the first flying bomb and ballistic missile, a host of wonder weapons, all of them too late and too few to make any difference,. The irony was that among the German Jews who fled to the United States in 1933 was Albert Einstein, later joined

ABOVE LEFT: *A Soviet political cartoon on Hitler's failure to take Moscow in 1941, recalling Napoleon's retreat from Moscow in the winter of 1812-13. Mussolini cowers behind the desk.*

LEFT: *Hitler and Mussolini at the height of their power only a year before. Center between them is Hitler's Deputy Führer, Rudolf Hess, who flew to Britain in a failed attempt to negotiate peace in 1941 and was imprisoned by the British.*

LEFT: *Hitler's birthday, 1942, showing him as he liked to appear to the German people. Even this early on in the war, some Germans had come to realise that Germany must eventually lose.*

BELOW: *Many of Hitler's generals blamed him for losing the war, but few were ready to oppose him. Here he confers about the Eastern Front with Wehrmacht Chief of Staff, Field Marshal Wilhelm Keitel and (right) Field Marshal Wilhelm von Leeb, who resigned his Army Group command in 1942, unable to cope with Hitler's interference. Hitler is holding the glasses he needed for reading, but refused to be photographed wearing.*

by other distinguished European physicists. If it had not been for his insistence on 'German science', Hitler might have had the atomic bomb.

On July 5th, 1943 Hitler began his last great attack in the east at the Battle of Kursk, the biggest tank battle in history, in an effort to shatter the Soviet line and with it their will to fight. In ten days the Germans were held and driven back with colossal losses, and the Eastern Front was doomed. On July 10th the British and Americans landed in Sicily, and within two weeks Mussolini was replaced by a new Italian government, which surrendered on September 3rd as the Allies invaded the Italian mainland, leaving the Germans to fight on alone. In September Hitler mounted a spectacular military rescue of his fellow dictator, and Mussolini became head of a German puppet state in north Italy.

Throughout the next winter Allied heavy bombers tore the heart out of Germany's major cities, and there was nothing but defeat on the battlefields. Hitler was by now visibly ill, brooding alone or ranting and storming at anyone who dared mention defeat or even negotiation. The new year was no better, with the Americans and British obviously preparing to invade France. Italy was out of the war, Japan visibly sinking, and there was nothing to stop the hordes on the Eastern Front. June 1944 turned out to be the fatal month. In Italy, the Allies broke through the German lines and liberated Rome, on June 6th they landed

ABOVE LEFT: *Hermann Göring in one of many flamboyant uniforms that he had designed for himself.*

ABOVE: *Hitler at his country house, the* Berghof *in Berchtesgaden, together with the estate gamekeepers. Hitler's favorite dog, Blondi, can also be seen.*

FAR LEFT: *Himmler with the notorious leader of the Norwegian puppet government set up by the Germans in 1940, Vikdung Quisling, who gave his name to all forms of collaboration with the enemy.*

LEFT: *Albert Speer inspects a captured Soviet T-34 tank in 1943. Despite Speer's own efforts, German tank production could not match its enemies' in quantity by this date.*

ABOVE LEFT: *Hitler visits his soldiers on the Eastern Front, 1944. By this date he had already told Martin Bormann that it was better for the German people all to die fighting than to live defeated.*

LEFT: *The shaken Hitler a few hours' after the assassination attempt, July 20th, 1944. The only physical injuries he suffered were bruises and damage to his hearing.*

in Normandy, and at the end of the month the Soviet 'Bagration' offensive took the Red Army to the borders of Poland. On July 20th a desperate conspiracy of German Army officers tried and failed to kill Hitler with a bomb in his headquarters.

After the failed bomb plot, the Gestapo and SS carried out a purge of Army officers. Even Rommel, who was slightly involved, was forced to commit suicide. The Nazi salute was made compulsory, and SS murder squads watched over the obedience of the Army and the nation. Only Hitler still continued to think of victory. In December 1944 he made a last fanciful attempt to break through the American defenses in the Ardennes, capture Antwerp, and cut off half the Allied forces in the west. The resulting 'Battle of the Bulge' only served to use up Germany's last reserves, and in January 1945 Soviet forces drove across Poland to within fifty miles of Berlin.

ABOVE: *Hitler shows Mussolini, who by coincidence visited his headquarters that day, the result of the bomb that so narrowly failed to kill him.*

Hitler had already moved to the Chancellery in Berlin, where he increasingly sought safety from the bombing in a secure bunker, finally not emerging at all. He was kept company by Eva Braun, by his dog, and by a few servants and hangers-on who could not believe that the Führer was finished. By this time Hitler was a broken man, perhaps clinically insane, still plotting his victories in a world that bore less and less resemblance to that outside. He made his last appearance above ground on April 20th, his fifty-sixth birthday. Of the Nazi leaders only Goebbels remained loyal, joining Hitler in the bunker on April 22nd. Six days later came news that Mussolini had been caught by Italian partisans and shot. Next day, with Soviet tanks only a few hundred yards away from his bunker, Hitler at last married Eva Braun, with Goebbels and Martin Bormann as witnesses. Hitler then wrote his 'political testament,' naming as his successor Admiral Karl Dönitz, the Commander-in-Chief of the Kriegsmarine, and gave orders for his dog to be destroyed. At 3.30pm on April 30th, 1945, his new wife took poison and Hitler shot himself. Then, following Hitler's last instructions, the two bodies were burned. On May 7th the forces of the Third Reich surrendered to their enemies.

FAR LEFT: *From his first days as Nazi Party leader Hitler kept a portrait of his idol Frederick the Great within sight. Even in 1945 he still hoped for victory.*

LEFT: *The remains of the bunker in the Chancellery garden where Hitler killed himself.*

BELOW LEFT: *The Reichstag building after its capture by Soviet troops.*

BELOW: *Soviet soldiers hoist the victory banner over the Reichstag, May 2nd, 1945.*

INDEX

Page numbers in *italics* refer to illustrations.

Acknowledgements

The publisher would like to thank Donald Somerville, who edited this book, Mike Rose, who designed it and Helen Dawson, who indexed it. We would also like to thank the German Bundesarchiv for supplying the majority of the illustrative material, and the following agencies and institutions for the remainder.

Bison Picture Library:
pages 1, 2-3, 8 (top), 28 (left), 29 (top and bottom), 32 (top), 33 (top), 36-37 (four), 40, 42 (top), 44-5 (four), 46 (upper right), 48-49 (five), 56 (top), 65 (bottom), 67 (top), 69 (bottom), 70 (bottom), 72 (top), 73 (bottom), 76 (top), 80

Center for the Study of Cartoons and Caricature, University of Kent at Canterbury: page 70 (top)

Imperial War Museum, London: pages 12, 13 (both), 15 (top), 16 (both), 17, 18-19, 55 (top), 58 (bottom), 59 (right), 76 (bottom)

Library of Congress, Washington: page 21

National Maritime Museum, Greenwich: page 59 (top)

Novosti Press Agency: page 77 (bottom)

US National Archives: page 62 (bottom)

WZ Bilddienst: page 55 (bottom)